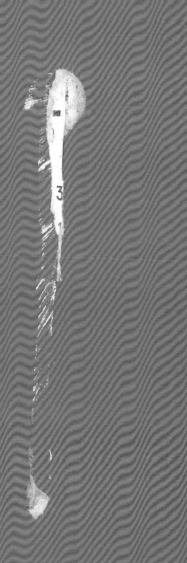

Call the
Police

Cath Senker

Photography by Howard Davies

W

FRANKLIN WATTS

LONDON•SYDNEY

This edition 2013

First published in 2010 by
Franklin Watts
338 Euston Road
London NW1 3BH

Franklin Watts Australia
Level 17/207 Kent Street
Sydney NSW 2000

Series editor: Julia Bird

Design: Nimbus Design

Photography: Howard Davies

A CIP catalogue record for this book is available
from the British Library.

ISBN 978 1 4451 1739 3

Dewey classification: 363.2

Printed in China

Franklin Watts is a division of Hachette Children's
Books, an Hachette UK company.
www.hachette.co.uk

Acknowledgements

The author and photographer would like to thank
the following for their help in the production of this
book: Sussex Police: PCSO Sharon Baker, Police
Constable James Conway, PC Georgie Edge, PCSO
Gill Everest, Sue Heard, PCSO David Hedgecock,
PC Vicky Jones, Sergeant Carl Knapp, PC Lizzie
Luckman, Sergeant Dave Palmer, PCSO John
Sharman, SC Martin Webb; PC Paul Ryder,
PC Beverly Webber, Ellie the Springer Spaniel and
the Gatwick Police Dog Unit; the staff of Brighton,
Hollingbury and Hove police stations and Brighton
Police CCTV Monitoring Unit. The National Black
Police Association: Stafford Brooks, Maurice Dando,
Che Donald. Sussex Police Helicopter: Amy Wright
and the pilots. We would also like to thank Sam
Foot, Sam Geering, Clive Hadwen, Jane Hawkins,
Joe Hedgecock, Shumaisa Khan, Vinod Mashru
(Bright News, Brighton), Lesley Norton, Clare
Pritchard, Kim Shaw; Jo Trotter and the children of
3Tr at Somerhill Junior School, Hove, East Sussex.

The photographs in this book feature police officers
and civilian models.

Cover picture: The police helicopter returns to base
after a job.

Contents

Words in **bold** can be found in the glossary
on page 28.

Call the police!

In some emergencies, people need to call the police. They call if there has been a crime, such as a **burglary**.

To ring the police in an emergency, call 999. Ask for the police. Remember to give your name and phone number. »

Police officers are always there to deal with emergencies. They work day or night **shifts**.

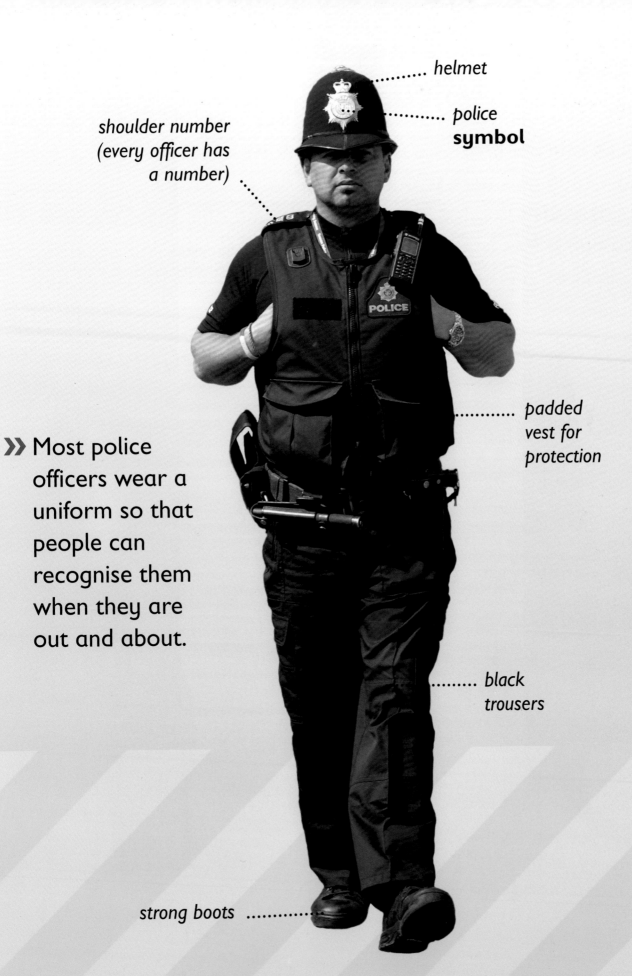

helmet

police **symbol**

shoulder number
(every officer has
a number)

padded
vest for
protection

>> Most police
officers wear a
uniform so that
people can
recognise them
when they are
out and about.

black
trousers

strong boots

Police equipment

Police officers always carry a **warrant card** to show they can **arrest** people. The dots are the words in **Braille**, for blind people. Police officers also carry lots of other equipment in their vest pockets or on their belt. **»**

Braille .·····

warrant card

torch to see in the dark

handcuffs *to* **restrain** *a* **suspect**

phone

>> The police have special equipment to protect them during **riots**.

baton

The helmet protects the head. It has the officer's number on it.

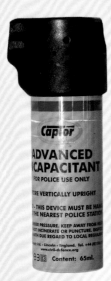

The police use **pepper spray** on people who are fighting them. They use it to stop a suspect from running away.

A riot shield protects the body during a fight.

Out on the beat

The police go out on the beat to try to prevent crime. The beat is their local area. Police officers walk, cycle or drive around it every day.

The police are often the first to arrive at an emergency, such as an accident. The officers try to deal with it. They may call the police station for help. »

A police car has a blue light that flashes in an emergency. This warns people to keep out of the way.

>> The police also **patrol** in busy places such as airports. They work with specially trained dogs that can sniff out **drugs** or **explosives**.

This dog sniffs bags at the airport to check for explosives.

Under arrest!

If police officers think someone has broken the **law**, they arrest the person. »

» This man is trying to steal from a shop. The shopkeeper spots him. He calls the police. »

>> Two police officers come straight away. They arrest the man and take him in a police car to the police station. An officer will ask him questions to find out what happened.

The officers want to restrain the suspect, so they put him in handcuffs.

At the custody centre

This woman has been arrested. She is taken to the police **custody centre**. She can call a friend or family member to say that she has been arrested. She may need a **lawyer**.

The suspect has to give her shoes, watch and money to a police officer. The police take her **fingerprints** (see page 23). Then the woman is locked in a cell. »

«« The cell is bare with just a bench to sit on.

A police officer interviews the suspect.

>> In the interview room, a police officer asks the woman questions about the crime. He takes notes so he can remember what she says. Sometimes interviews may also be recorded.

Road police

The road police check that people are driving safely and not too fast. They use special equipment to check how fast cars are going. »

This hand-held device measures speed.

» Road police cars have a camera on top. It takes photos of car number plates. The police use the photos to track down drivers who have been caught speeding. They also look for cars that have been stolen or used in a crime. »

» If people have drunk alcohol, it is dangerous to drive. Officers stop drivers who they think might be drunk. They give them a **breath test**.

An officer carries out a breath test on a driver to see if she has been drinking alcohol.

Emergency!
Road accident

Police officers are often the first people to arrive after a road accident. They carry a **first aid** pouch. Officers are trained to save people's lives.

If a person is badly hurt in a road accident, it can be quickest to take them to hospital in the police helicopter. »

A helicopter can travel faster than an ambulance.

>> This cyclist has been hit by a car. The police officer checks first that she has no broken bones. Then she asks the cyclist what happened. >>

>> The officer also talks to a **witness** to the accident. The **statements** from witnesses may be used in **court** to help decide who was to blame for the accident.

Crowd control

At big events, such as football matches or **protests**, the police keep order. They check that no one is carrying a **weapon**. They also watch out for thieves.

The police are ready if there is an emergency. If a fight breaks out between different groups, they separate them. If there is violence, they may arrest the people who are fighting. »

Mounted police (on horseback) can move fast in an emergency.

>> Police officers also help to look for missing people. It does not happen often, but sometimes children become lost in crowds or busy places. A Police **Community** Support Officer (see page 24) helps this boy to find his mum.

Look for a police officer if you are lost in a crowded place.

Police technology

The police use many kinds of **technology** to help keep people safe and to find criminals.

They use **CCTV** cameras to record what happens in busy places, such as shopping centres. If the cameras record a crime, the pictures will help the police to find the suspects. »

A police officer uses CCTV to check what is happening on the streets.

>> The police also take fingerprints at **crime scenes**. Everyone has different fingerprints.

The police scan suspects' fingerprints on a computer. They try to match them to fingerprints at the crime scene. >>

A police officer takes a suspect's fingerprints. >>>>

>> The police also use **DNA** to help them track down criminals. A spot of blood or a hair at a crime scene contains the DNA of the person who left it.

Police Community Support Officers

Police Community Support Officers (PCSOs) support the work of police officers. They help to direct traffic and control crowds. PCSOs also give advice to people in the community on how to stay safe. »

These PCSOs visit a shopping centre so that people can talk to them about problems in their area.

>> PCSOs deal with minor crimes, such as dumped cars, graffiti and litter. They cannot arrest people.

Two PCSOs talk to some young people. They ask them if they know who painted this graffiti.

Doing the right thing

School liaison officers visit local schools to tell children about the work that the police do. They also help children to learn right from wrong. »

The officer is asking these children what they would do if they saw a crime.

The officer is showing the children what to do if they find a bag on the street.

>> School liaison officers also advise children on how to stay safe. Here are some good rules to follow:

- Learn your home phone number or write it down and keep it with you.

- If you are lost, talk to a safe adult, such as a police officer or a PCSO.

- Never go anywhere with a stranger.

Glossary

arrest
To take someone to the police station.

baton
A short thick stick that the police carry as a weapon.

burglary
Breaking into a place to steal things.

Braille
Writing that uses raised dots so that blind people can read them by touching the letters.

breath test
To take a breath test, a person breathes into a device. It shows if he or she has drunk alcohol.

CCTV
A TV system that records what happens in an area.

community
People who live in the same area.

court
The place where people decide if another person has carried out a crime.

crime scene
The place where a crime takes place.

custody centre
The place where the police take people they have arrested so they can ask them questions.

DNA
The chemical in the cells of the body that has genes, which make you how you are.

drugs
Chemicals that change the way your body works.

explosives
Something that blows up.

fingerprint
The mark made by the pattern of lines on a fingertip.

first aid
Emergency help given to a person who is ill or hurt.

handcuffs
A pair of metal rings that are locked around a suspect's hands.

law
The rules of a country that everyone must obey.

lawyer
A person who is trained in the law and can give advice to suspects.

patrol
To walk or travel around an area to protect it.

pepper spray
A gas that stings the eyes and makes you cough.

protest
An action people take if they are angry about something that has happened.

restrain
To keep someone or something under control.

riot
When a crowd behaves in a violent way, as a protest.

shift
The time that people work, such as from 8 a.m. to 8 p.m.

statement
When people make a statement to the police about a crime, they tell them what happened.

suspect
Someone who the police think has carried out a crime.

symbol
An object that stands for something.

technology
Using science to help you make and do things.

warrant card
A card that shows that a police officer can arrest people.

weapon
Something that can hurt people, such as a knife.

witness
A person who saw a crime and tells the police what happened.

Finding out more

Books

People Who Help Us: The Police by Clare Oliver (Franklin Watts, 2007)

Police Officers on Patrol by Kersten Hamilton (Viking Children's Books, 2009)

Popcorn: People Who Help Us: Police by Adam Sutherland (Wayland, 2010)

When I'm at Work: Police Officer by Sue Barraclough (Franklin Watts, 2011)

Websites

Kids Aware
www.gloucestershire.police.uk/kids_aware/1.html
Gloucestershire Police website with information for young people about how to stay safe.

Safe Street
www.safestreet.info/
About the role of police officers, health and safety information and citizenship advice. Includes quizzes and videos.

Station Kids
www.spstation.com/kids/index.php
All about the police force, safety and the law.

Note to parents and teachers: every effort has been made by the Publishers to ensure that these websites are suitable for children, that they are of the highest educational value, and that they contain no inappropriate or offensive material. However, because of the nature of the Internet, it is impossible to guarantee that the contents of these sites will not be altered. We strongly advise that Internet access is supervised by a responsible adult.

Index